331 Great Quotes for Entrepreneurs:
You Dream, You Believe, You Create & You Succeed

Edited by Axel Tracy

I0462564

Text Copyright © 2013 Bidi Capital Pty Ltd
All rights reserved.

Disclaimer:
The material in this publication (the "book") and the information accessed through it is of a general nature only and does not contain investment recommendations or professional advice. The information is not to be relied upon as being accurate, complete or up to date. Axel Tracy (the "editor") and Bidi Capital Pty Ltd (the "publisher") recommends that, before acting or not acting upon information contained or referred to in this book, readers should seek independent professional advice that takes into account their financial situation, investment objectives, particular needs and/or other personal circumstances. The information contained in this book is not to be used for any purpose other than a quotation reference and it is not to be construed as an indication or prediction of future results from any investment. Axel Tracy and Bidi Capital Pty Ltd do not offer financial or business. To the maximum extent permitted by law, the editor and publisher disclaim all responsibility and liability to any person, arising from directly or indirectly from any person taking or not taking action based upon the information in this publication.

For Richard, Muhammad, Andrew, Paul, Warren, Roger, Mark & Steve: Thanks all the entrepreneurship inspiration and drive you gave me: if I only I can become half as successful as any of you.

Table of Contents

About the Editor

Axel Tracy is an accounting and business student at the University of Technology, Sydney. He has a passion for his studies and has been accepted into the invitation-only Golden Key International Honours Society in recognition of having a GPA that placed him in the top bracket of students at his university.

He was until recently also employed by the University of Technology, Sydney, to run PASS sessions in the subject of Accounting Standards and Regulations; an undergraduate accounting subject that trains students to become familiar with Australia's implementation of International Financial Reporting Standards and the current Australian accounting standard regime.

Since April, 2011, he has been the Founder & Director of Bidi Capital Pty Ltd, a holding company with two internet businesses revolving around accounting & finance (accofina.com & RatioAnalysis.net). Bidi Capital has had average quarterly revenue growth of 194% over the past two years.

Axel lives in inner city Sydney, Australia.

About accofina.com

accofina.com was launched in September, 2013, and is a hub for accounting & finance knowledge and technology. On the website you will find Kindle eBooks, iOS Apple Apps & MS Excel Spreadsheets all customized to assist putting academic accounting & finance knowledge, through technology, in the hands of businesspeople and investors.accofina.com is part of Bidi Capital Pty Ltd, which is a company founded, directed and owned by this book's editor, Axel Tracy.

Introduction

So here you go, you want to be or are already an entrepreneur. It's a tough but highly rewarding journey that will involve creating your own path by forcing yourself out of your comfort zone. While the benefits are limitless you are going to need certain skills to help you achieve your dreams, and part of gaining those skills will require inspiration, motivation and direction to get you there.

This book has drawn upon the wisdom of some of history's greatest entrepreneurs, leaders & thinkers and packaged their knowledge into easily digestible quotations that you can refer to in your entrepreneurship journey and dream fulfillment.

The book has been broken down into twelve categories, or chapters, that each cover particular traits and skills found in successful entrepreneurs. You can jump to whatever category you need guidance with and need not necessarily read from beginning to end in a direct line. Each category has a very brief 'Editor's note' to begin with that introduces the topic, but then it is straight into it with the quotations, their source and the source's one-line bio.

I hope you find this book as enjoyable to read (and later refer to) as I did in editing it, in fact as I continued my own business while putting together this book I used it and the quotes inside to guide me in my own entrepreneurship path when I was stuck a few times.

If you want to help me with a second edition, please email me at **axel@accofina.com** and give me your suggestions. If you want to help me become a best-selling publisher, please leave a positive review for this book (and maybe a comment on how this book helped you) on Amazon.com.

Let's leave my input behind and start getting into the quotes and get inspired!

Best wishes for your business!

Self-belief & Attitude

Editor's Note:
As you are most likely well aware, to become and entrepreneur and reach a successful stage you be will often face negative thinking from others as well as your own self-doubt along the way. To have the right mind-set to overcome these obstacles is critical. You will be taking a less trodden path and leaving your comfort zone and you must learn to have the self-belief and right attitude that will keep you moving from point A to B to C, all the way to success. These quotes help to shape these qualities and allow you to have the right level of confidence about your journey.

"A pessimist sees the difficulty in every opportunity; an optimist sees the opportunity in every difficulty."
Winston Churchill *(1874 – 1965) British prime minister*

"All that we are is a result of what we have thought."
Gautama Buddha *(563 – 483 BCE) The "enlightened one" of Buddhism*

"We have it in our power to begin the world over again."
Thomas Paine *(1737 – 1808) English-American author, political activist & theorist*

"Our life is what our thoughts make it."
Marcus Aurelius *(121 – 180) Roman emperor*

"What we can or cannot do, what we consider possible or impossible, is rarely a function of our true capability. It is more likely a function of our beliefs about who we are."
Anthony Robbins *(1960 -) American life coach & motivational speaker*

"The secret of making something work in your lives is, first of all, the deep desire to make it work: then the faith and belief that it can work: then to hold that clear definite vision in your consciousness and see it working out step by step, without one thought of doubt or disbelief."
Eileen Caddy *(1917 – 2006) American spiritual writer & teacher*

"One person with a belief is equal to a force of ninety-nine who have only interests."
John Stuart Mill *(1806-1873) British economist & philosopher*

"Clouds come floating into my life, no longer to carry rain or usher storm, but to add color to my sunset sky."
Rabindranath Tagore *(1861-1941) Indian poet & philosopher*

"I believe the choice to be excellent begins with aligning your thoughts and words with the intention to require more from yourself."
Oprah Winfrey *(1954 -) American founder & CEO Harpo Productions & Oprah Winfrey Network*

"The only limit to our realization of tomorrow will be our doubts of today."
Franklin D. Roosevelt *(1882-1945) American president*

"The longer I live, the more I realize the impact of attitude on life. Attitude, to me, is more important than facts. It is more important than the past, the education, the money, than circumstances, than failure, than successes, than what other people think or say or do. It is more important than appearance, giftedness or skill. It will make or break a company... a church... a home. The remarkable thing is we have a choice everyday regarding the attitude we will embrace for that day. We cannot change our past... we cannot change the fact that people will act in a certain way. We cannot change the inevitable. The only thing we can do is play on the one string we have, and that is our attitude. I am convinced that life is 10% what happens to me and 90% of how I react to it. And so it is with you... we are in charge of our Attitudes."
Charles R. Swindoll *(1934 -) American pastor & author*

"Believe in yourself! Have faith in your abilities! Without a humble but reasonable confidence in your own powers you cannot be successful or happy."
Norman Vincent Peale *(1898 – 1993) American minister & author*

"A man cannot be comfortable without his own approval."
Mark Twain *(1835 – 1910) American author & humourist*

"Whether you think you can or think you can't - you are right."

—

Henry Ford *(1863 – 1947) American founder of the Ford Motor Company*

"To be a great champion you must believe you are the best. If you're not, pretend you are."
Muhammad Ali *(1942 -) American boxer*

"A man is but the product of his thoughts; what he thinks, he becomes."
Mahatma Gandhi *(1869 – 1948) Indian political and spiritual leader*

"I was always looking outside myself for strength and confidence, but it comes from within. It is there all the time."
Anna Freud *(1895 – 1982) Austrian psychiatrist*

"Whatever you do, be different – that was the advice my mother gave me, and I can't think of better advice for an entrepreneur. If you're different, you will stand out."
Anita Roddick *(1942 – 2007) British founder of The Body Shop*

"A happy person is not a person in a certain set of circumstances, but rather a person with a certain set of attitudes."
Hugh Downs *(1921 -) American broadcaster & anchor*

"When you change the way you look at things, the things you look at change."
Max Planck *Nobel Prize-winning physicist*

"Whether you think you can or think you can't - you are right."
Henry Ford *(1863 – 1947) American founder of the Ford Motor Company*

"A cloudy day is no match for a sunny disposition."
William Arthur Ward *(1921 – 1994) American author*

"Attitude is a little thing that makes a big difference."
Winston Churchill *(1874 – 1965) British prime minister*

"Happiness is not by chance, but by choice."
Jim Rohn *(1930 – 2009) American motivational speaker & author*

"Faith is to believe what we do not see; and the reward of this faith is to see what we believe."
St. Augustine *(354 – 430) Numidian Christian theologian*

"I never saw a pessimistic general win a battle."
Dwight D. Eisenhower *(1890 – 1969) American president*

"It's lack of faith that makes people afraid of meeting challenges, and I believe in myself."
Muhammad Ali *(1942 -) American boxer*

"The barrier between success is not something which exists in the real world: it is composed purely and simply of doubts about ability."
Franklin D. Roosevelt *(1882-1945) American president*

"If we did all the things we were capable of doing, we would literally astound ourselves."
Thomas Edison *(1847 – 1931) American inventor and businessperson*

"Whatever you do, be different – that was the advice my mother gave me, and I can't think of better advice for an entrepreneur. If you're different, you will stand out."
Anita Roddick *(1942 – 2007) British founder of The Body Shop*

"A cloudy day is no match for a sunny disposition."
William Arthur Ward *(1921 – 1994) American author*

"Your attitude is more important that your aptitude."
Zig Ziglar *(1926 – 2012) American salesman, author & motivational speaker*

"Logic will get you from A to B. Imagination will take you everywhere."
Albert Einstein *(1879 – 1955) Swiss-American Nobel-laureate physicist*

"The only victory that counts is the one over yourself."
Jesse Owens *American Sprinter and Long Jumper*

"Life is like a wild tiger. You can either lie down and let it lay its paw on your head--or sit on its back and ride it."

Ruth Tearle *South African author and businessperson*

"Laugh at yourself, but don't ever aim your doubt at yourself. Be bold. When you embark for strange places, don't leave any of yourself safely on shore. Have the nerve to go into unexplored territory."
Alan Alda *(1936 -) American actor & director*

"If you don't like something, change it. If you can't change it, change your attitude."
Maya Angelou *(1928 -) American author & poet*

"Somehow I can't believe that there are any heights that can't be scaled by a man who knows the secrets of making dreams come true. This special secret, it seems to me, can be summarized in four C s. They are curiosity, confidence, courage, and constancy, and the greatest of all is confidence. When you believe in a thing, believe in it all the way, implicitly and unquestionable."
Walt Disney *(1901 – 1966) American founder The Walt Disney Company*

"The barrier between success is not something which exists in the real world: it is composed purely and simply of doubts about ability."
Franklin D. Roosevelt *(1882-1945) American president*

"Fearlessness is like a muscle. I know from my own life that the more I exercise it the more natural it becomes to not let my fears run me."
Arianna Huffington *(1950 -) Greek-American founder of The Huffington Post*

Focus & Goal Orientation

Editor's Note:
You will soon find (if you haven't already) that your task list can quickly balloon into an unmanageable mess. Often competing interests will pull you in different directions. To become a successful entrepreneur you must have the ability to efficiently manage your time so you are achieving what you originally set out to do and not being pulled off course. You must keep an eye on the long-term and match that to the immediate short-term tasks to get there. These quotes will both inspire and remind you on how to keep focused, driven and use goal-setting to reach your overall objectives.

"No one is free who does not lord over himself."
Claudius *(10 BCE – 54 AD) Roman emperor*

"We are too busy mopping the floor to turn off the faucet."
Unknown

"One of the strongest characteristics of genius is the power of lighting its own fire."
John W. Foster *(1836 – 1917) American colonel & diplomat*

"My success, part of it certainly, is that I have focused in on a few things."
Bill Gates *(1955 -) American founder of Microsoft and The Bill & Melinda Gates Foundation*

"Every single life only becomes great when the individual sets upon a goal or goals which they really believe in, which they can really commit themselves to, which they can put their whole heart and soul into."
Brian Tracy *(1944 -) Canadian author & motivational speaker*

"You have to know what you want to get."
Gertrude Stein *(1874 – 1946) American writer*

"Every man's life lies within the present; for the past is spent and done with, and the future is uncertain."

Marcus Aurelius *(121 – 180) Roman emperor*

"It's only by saying 'no' that you can concentrate on the things that are really important."
Steve Jobs *(1955 – 2011) American founder of Apple, Pixar & NeXT*

"Energy is the essence of life. Every day you decide how you're going to use it by knowing what you want and what it takes to reach that goal, and by maintaining focus."
Oprah Winfrey *(1954 -) Founder & CEO Harpo Productions & Oprah Winfrey Network*

"Dream as if you'll live forever, live as if you'll die today."
James Dean *(1931 – 1955) American actor*

"Avoid fragmentation: Find your focus and seek simplicity. Purposeful living calls for elegant efficiency and economy of effort—expending the minimum time and energy necessary to achieve desired goals."
Dan Millman *(1946 -) American author and motivational speaker*

"The tragedy in life doesn't lie in not reaching your goal. The tragedy lies in having no goal to reach."
Benjamin Mays *(1894 – 1984) American minister, educator & social activist*

"As long as you are going to be thinking anyway, think big."
Donald Trump *(1946 -) American founder of The Trump Organisation and Trump Entertainment Resorts*

"Often he who does too much does too little."
Italian proverb

"Whatever we put our attention on will grow stronger in our life."
Maharishi Mahesh Yogi *(1918 – 2008) Indian spiritual leader*

"A goal is a dream with a deadline."
Napoleon Hill *(1883 – 1970) American author & motivational speaker*

"The critical ingredient is getting off your butt and doing something. It's as simple as that. A lot of people have ideas, but there are few who decide to do something about them now. Not tomorrow. Not

next week. But today. The true entrepreneur is a doer, not a dreamer."
Nolan Bushnell *(1943 -) American founder of Atari and Chuck E. Cheese's Pizza Time Theatre*

"You are never too old to set another goal or to dream a new dream."
C.S. Lewis *(1898 – 1963) Northern Irish author & academic*

"You need to have a passionate interest in why things are happening. That cast of mind, kept over long periods, gradually improves your ability to focus on reality. If you don't have the cast of mind, you're destined for failure even if you have a high I.Q."
Charlie Munger *(1924 -) American investor, Vice-Chairman Berkshire Hathaway & Chairman Wesco Financial*

"I'm a great believer in luck, and I find the harder I work, the more luck I have."
Thomas Jefferson *(1743 – 1826) American president and independence leader*

"One day you can be a kid, but another day you have to be like this is your job, you play tennis. You have to work for that."
Martina Hingis *(1980 -) Swiss tennis player*

"You must have long term goals to keep you from being frustrated by short term failures."
Unknown

"Drive thy business or it will drive thee."
Benjamin Franklin *(1706 - 1790) American president & polymath*

"All personal achievements start in your mind. The first step is to know exactly what your problem, goal or desire is."
W. Clement Stone *(1902 – 2002) American author & businessperson*

"Goals determine what you're going to be."
Julius Erving *(1950 -) American basketballer*

"My interest in life comes from setting myself huge, apparently unachievable challenges and trying to rise above them."
Richard Branson *(1950 -) British founder of Virgin Group*

"Fix your eyes forward on what you can do, not back on what you cannot change."
Tom Clancy *(1947 -) American author*

"The greatest danger for most of us is not that our aim is too high and we miss it, but that it is too low and we reach it."
Michelangelo *(1475 – 1564) Italian artist*

Leadership & Management

Editor's Note:
Depending on how quickly your business grows and the level of
influence you and your business have, you will soon how the
responsibility of being a leader and manager. The skillsets required
here involve personal characteristics as well as management science
techniques. Without quickly picking up adequate leadership and
management skills you may find your growth is limited or that you
have an unproductive and unhappy team. These quotes harness the
knowledge of many successful leaders and managers and give you
bite-sized advice on how you can become a great leader and
manager yourself.

"Every employee, not just the senior people, should know how a
company is doing."
Jack Welch *(1935 -) American businessperson*

"If you can run one business well, you can run any business well."
Richard Branson *(1950 -) British founder of Virgin Group*

"Undoubtedly a man is to labour to better his condition, but first to
better himself"
William Ellery Channing *(1780 – 1842) American preacher*

"One kind word can warm three winter months."
Japanese Proverb

"To reform a world, to reform a nation, no wise man will undertake;
and all but foolish men know, that the only solid, though a far slower
reformation, is what each begins and perfects on himself."
Thomas Carlyle *(1795 – 1881) Scottish philosopher*

"Sometimes, I think my most important job as a CEO is to listen for
bad news. If you don't act on it, your people will eventually stop
bringing bad news to your attention and that is the beginning of the
end."
Bill Gates *(1955 -) American founder of Microsoft and The Bill &
Melinda Gates Foundation*

"Focus on all four of your net worth factors: increasing your income, increasing your savings, increasing your investment returns, and decreasing your cost of living by simplifying your lifestyle."
T. Harv Eker *(1954 -) Canadian author & motivational speaker*

"Wall Street people learn nothing and forget everything."
Benjamin Graham *(1894 – 1976) American investor & academic*

"Leadership is a potent combination of strategy and character. But if you must be without one, be without the strategy."
Norman Schwarzkopf *(1934 – 2012) American general*

"We must be the change we wish to see."
Mahatma Gandhi *(1869 – 1948) Indian political and spiritual leader*

"Leadership and learning are indispensable to each other."
John F. Kennedy *(1917 – 1963) American president*

"Man's biggest mistake is to believe that he's working for someone else."
Unknown

"Vision without execution is hallucination."
Thomas Edison *(1847 – 1931) American inventor and businessperson*

"Do not follow where the path may lead. Go instead where there is no path and leave a trail."
Ralph Waldo Emerson *(1803 – 1882) American writer & lecturer*

"No man will make a great leader who wants to do it all himself, or to get all the credit for doing it."
Andrew Carnegie *(1835 – 1919) Scottish-American founder of Carnegie Steel Company & philanthropist*

"Innovation has nothing to do with how many R&D dollars you have. When Apple came up with the Mac, IBM was spending at least 100 times more on R&D. It's not about money. It's about the people you have, and how you're led."
Steve Jobs *(1955 – 2011) American founder of Apple, Pixar & NeXT*

"Try not to be a man of success, but rather try to become a man of value."
Albert Einstein *(1879 – 1955) Swiss-American Nobel-laureate physicist*

"Fit no stereotypes. Don't chase the latest management fads. The situation dictates which approach best accomplishes the team's mission."
Colin Powell *(1937 -) American general & statesperson*

"An excuse is worse and more terrible than a lie, for an excuse is a lie guarded."
John Paul I *(1912 – 1978) Italian Roman Catholic Pope*

"Budgets are for cutting, that's why you set them."
Laurence Buckman *British doctor*

"An army of lions commanded by a deer will never be an army of lions."
Napoleon Bonaparte *(1769 – 1821) French emperor*

"Strategy gets you on the playing field, but execution pays the bills."
Gordon Eubanks *(1946 -) American founder of Compiler Systems and businessperson*

"Go to the people. Learn from them. Live with them. Start with what they know. Build with what they have. The best of leaders when the job is done, when the task is accomplished, the people will say we have done it ourselves."
Lao Tzu *Chinese Zhou dynasty philosopher*

"It takes 20 years to build a reputation and five minutes to ruin it. If you think about that, you'll do things differently."
Warren Buffett *(1930 -) American investor & Chairman Berkshire Hathaway*

"I suppose that leadership at one time meant muscle; but today it means getting along with people."
Indira Gandhi *(1917 – 1984) Indian prime minister*

"The best executive is the one who has sense enough to pick good men to do what he wants done, and self-restraint to keep from

meddling with them while they do it."
Theodore Roosevelt *(1858 – 1919) American president*

"When a management team with a reputation for brilliance tackles a business with a reputation for bad economics, it is the reputation of the business that remains intact."
Warren Buffett *(1930 -) American investor & Chairman Berkshire Hathaway*

"When you're finished changing, you're finished."
Benjamin Franklin *(1706 - 1790) American president & polymath*

"Remember the difference between a boss and a leader. A boss says, Go! A leader says, Let's go!"
Unknown

"A leader leads by example not by force."
Sun Tzu *(544 – 496 BCE) Chinese general*

"Too many leaders act as if the sheep… their people… are there for the benefit of the shepherd, not that the shepherd has responsibility for the sheep."
Ken Blanchard *(1939 -) American author and businessperson*

"The most elusive and desired quality of leadership is vision. Vision is the perfume of the mind."
Harriet Rubin *(1953 -) American writer*

"The person who figures out how to harness the collective genius of his or her organization is going to blow the competition away."
Walter Wriston *(1919 – 2005) American banker*

Persistence & Fortitude

Editor's Note:
It's almost guaranteed you will face failures and setbacks in your entrepreneurial journey. As many successful entrepreneurs say, it's important to overcome these immediate hurdles and not be stopped in your tracks. The ability to persist while facing difficulties is a key trait needed for any new entrepreneur. With this ability you will be able to turn short-term failures into long-term success. These quotes hope to reinforce your personal strength and give you the fortitude to press on.

"Obstacles cannot crush me. Every obstacle yields to stern resolve. He who is fixed to a star does not change his mind."
Leonardo da Vinci *(1452 – 1519) Italian artist & polymath*

"Do not fear mistakes. You will know failure. Continue to reach out."
Robert Galvin *(1922 – 2011) American businessperson*

"Business opportunities are like buses, there's always another one coming."
Richard Branson *(1950 -) British founder of Virgin Group*

"If I had to select one quality, one personal characteristic that I regard as being most highly correlated with success, whatever the field, I would pick the trait of persistence. Determination. The will to endure to the end, to get knocked down seventy times and get up off the floor saying, 'Here comes number seventy-one!'"
Richard M. DeVos *(1926 -) American founder of Amway*

"History is made at night. Character is what you are in the dark."
Lord John Whorfin *Fictional character from 'Buckaroo Banzai' (1984)*

"Entrepreneurship is living a few years of your life like most people won't, so that you can spend the rest of your life like most people can't."
Unknown

"Let my name stand among those who are willing to bear ridicule and reproach for the truth's sake, and so earn some right to rejoice when

the victory is won."
Louisa May Alcott *(1832 – 1888) American writer*

"To be nobody but yourself in a world which is doing its best, day and night, to make you like everybody else is to fight the hardest battle which any human being can fight...but never stop fighting!"
E.E. Cummings *(1894 – 1962) American writer*

"We acquire the strength we have overcome."
Ralph Waldo Emerson *(1803 – 1882) American writer & lecturer*

"Success is walking from failure to failure with no loss of enthusiasm."
Winston Churchill *(1874 – 1965) British prime minister*

"Strength does not come from physical capacity. It comes from an indomitable will."
Mahatma Gandhi *(1869 – 1948) Indian political and spiritual leader*

"Refuse to throw in the towel. Go that extra mile that failures refuse to travel. It is far better to be exhausted from success than to be rested from failure."
Mary Kay Ash *(1918 – 2001) American founder of Mary Kay Cosmetics*

"The ultimate measure of a man is not where he stands in moments of comfort, but where he stands at times of challenge and controversy."
Martin Luther King Jr. *(1929-1968) American civil rights leader & Nobel Peace Prize laureate*

"Success is how high you bounce after you hit bottom."
George S. Patton *(1885 – 1945) American general*

"I am a slow walker, but I never walk back."
Abraham Lincoln *(1808 – 1865) American president*

"Obstacles can't stop you. Problems can't stop you. Most of all, other people can't stop you. Only you can stop you."
Jeffrey Gomer *(1946 -) American author & lecturer*

"When everything seems to be going against you, remember that the airplane takes off against the wind, not with it."

Henry Ford *(1863 – 1947) American founder of the Ford Motor Company*

"I knew that if I failed I wouldn't regret that, but I knew the one thing I might regret is not trying."
Jeff Bezos *(1964 -) American founder of Amazon.com*

"I've missed more than 9000 shots in my career. I've lost almost 300 games. 26 times, I've been trusted to take the game winning shot and missed. I've failed over and over and over again in my life. And that is why I succeed."
Michael Jordan *(1963 -) American basketballer*

"It's not the size of the dog in the fight, it's the size of the fight in the dog."
Mark Twain *(1835 – 1910) American author & humourist*

"A man who wakes up and finds himself a success hasn't been asleep."
Dave Thomas *(1932 – 2002) American founder of Wendy's*

"Don't worry about failure; you only have to be right once."
Drew Houston *(1983 -) American founder of Dropbox*

"Ambition is the path to success. Persistence is the vehicle you arrive in."
Bill Bradley *(1943 -) American basketballer & senator*

"Every worthwhile accomplishment, big or little, has its stages of drudgery and triumph; a beginning, a struggle and a victory."
Mahatma Gandhi *(1869 – 1948) Indian political and spiritual leader*

"Victory is always possible for the person who refuses to stop fighting."
Napoleon Hill *(1883 – 1970) American author & motivational speaker*

"In the depth of winter, I finally learned that within me there lay an invincible summer."
Albert Camus *(1913 – 1960) French writer, philosopher & Nobel laureate*

"Victory is sweetest when you've known defeat."
Malcolm Forbes *(1919 – 1990) American publisher*

"Nobody trips over mountains. It is the small pebble that causes you to stumble. Pass all the pebbles in your path and you will find that you have crossed the mountain."
Unknown

"Fall down seven times. Stand up eight."
Japanese proverb

"Eighty percent of success is showing up."
Woody Allen *(1935 -) American actor & director*

"The best way out is always through."
Robert Frost *(1874 – 1963) American poet*

Communication & Teamwork

Editor's Note:
Being able to communicate well and build your team are two qualities required if any business is going to grow beyond the size of the entrepreneur. For some this may be very easy, but for others it may be a little more unnatural, or at least when it comes to working in a team, different from when the business was yours alone. Regardless of where you sit on this spectrum, these quotes will hopefully make you a better communicator and team builder and member.

"Behind every able man, there are always other able men."
Chinese Proverb

"If I have seen farther than others, it is because I was standing on the shoulder of giants."
Isaac Newton *(1642 – 1727) English physicist & mathematician*

"I have often regretted my speech, never my silence."
Xenocrates *(396 – 314 BCE) Greek philosopher & mathematician*

"The basic difference between being assertive and being aggressive is how our words and behavior affect the rights and well being of others."
Sharon A. Bower *Author*

"Words are, of course, the most powerful drug used by mankind."
Rudyard Kipling *(1865 – 1936) English writer*

"We never listen when we are eager to speak."
François de La Rochefoucauld *(1613 – 1680) French writer*

"If two men on the same job agree all the time, then one is useless. If they disagree all the time, both are useless."
Darryl F. Zanuck *(1902 – 1979) American producer*

"We must all hang together, or assuredly, we shall all hang separately."

Benjamin Franklin *(1706 - 1790) American president & polymath*

"When he took time to help the man up the mountain, lo, he scaled it himself."
Tibetan Proverb

"The most important thing in communication is to hear what isn't being said."
Peter Drucker *(1909 – 2005) American author & educator*

"None of us is as smart as all of us."
Ken Blanchard *(1939 -) American author and businessperson*

"Two monologues do not make a dialogue."
Jeff Daly *American designer*

"In the long history of humankind (and animal kind, too) those who learned to collaborate and improvise most effectively have prevailed."
Charles Darwin *(1809 – 1882) English naturalist*

"You can talk all day, and say nothing."
Jack Ryan *Fictional character in Tom Clancy novels*

"Never doubt that a small group of thoughtful, committed people can change the world. Indeed, it is the only thing that ever has."
Margaret Mead *(1901 – 1978) American anthropologist*

"Electric communication will never be a substitute for the face of someone who with their soul encourages another person to be brave and true."
Charles Dickens *(1812 – 1870) English writer*

"It is only as we develop others that we permanently succeed."
Harvey S. Firestone *(1868-1938) Founder Of Firestone Tire And Rubber Company*

"Silence is a source of great strength."
Lao Tzu *Chinese Zhou dynasty philosopher*

"You can have brilliant ideas, but if you can't get them across, your ideas won't get you anywhere."

Lee Iacocca *(1924 -) American businessperson*

"A boat doesn't go forward if each one is rowing their own way."
Swahili proverb

"You don't become a great team overnight, no matter how much money you have at your disposal."
Frank Lampard *(1978 -) English footballer*

"Wise men talk because they have something to say; fools because they have to say something."
Plato *(428 – 348 BCE) Greek philosopher & mathematician*

"It is better to have one person working with you than three people working for you."
Dwight D. Eisenhower *(1890 – 1969) American president*

"When was ever honey made with one bee in a hive?"
Thomas Hood *(1799 – 1845) British humourist & poet*

"There are few, if any, jobs in which ability alone is sufficient. Needed, also, are loyalty, sincerity, enthusiasm and team play."
William B. Given, Jr. *Author*

"A group becomes a team when each member is sure enough of himself and his contribution to praise the skill of the others."
Unknown

"The five separate fingers are five independent units. Close them and the fist multiplies strength. This is organization."
James Cash Penney *(1875 – 1971) American founder of J. C. Penney*

Selling & Customer Service

Editor's Note:
This skill-set is another that divides a lot of entrepreneurs: you were either born to do it or it frightens the hell out of you. But the bottom line is that great selling and customer service skills are a must for any entrepreneur. You will need to sell your business to financiers, your supporters (including family) and then ultimately to your clients…and then you need to be able to keep your clients as repeat business over the long-term. These quotes will build your confidence and shape your attitude towards this fundamental skill-set.

"Don't open a shop unless you like to smile."
Chinese Proverb

"You don't close a sale, you open a relationship if you want to build a long-term, successful enterprise."
Patricia Fripp *Author & lecturer*

"There is only one boss. The customer. And he can fire everybody in the company from the chairman on down, simply by spending his money somewhere else."
Sam Walton *(1918 – 1992) American founder of Wal-Mart*

"My greatest challenge has been to change the mindset of people. Mindsets play strange tricks on us. We see things the way our minds have instructed our eyes to see."
Muhammad Yunus *(1940 -) Bangladeshi banker, economist & Nobel Peace Prize laureate*

"Communication is everyone's panacea for everything."
Tom Peters *(1942 -) American writer*

"Good customer service costs less than bad customer service."
Sally Gronow *British businessperson*

"Customers don't expect you to be perfect. They do expect you to fix things when they go wrong."
Donald Porter *British businessperson*

"Make a customer, not a sale."
Katherine Barchetti *American businessperson*

"In the world of internet customer service, it is important to remember your competitor is only a mouse click away."
Unknown

"If you work just for money, you'll never make it. But if you love what you are doing, and always put the customer first, success will be yours."
Ray Kroc *(1902 – 1984) American McDonalds Inc. pioneer & franchisor*

"Well done is better than well said."
Benjamin Franklin *(1706 - 1790) American president & polymath*

"There are no traffic jams along the extra mile."
Roger Staubach *(1942 -) American footballer & businessperson*

"The most unprofitable item ever manufactured is an excuse."
John Mason *Author & minister*

"If you do build a great experience, customers tell each other about that. Word of mouth is very powerful."
Jeff Bezos *(1964 -) American founder of Amazon.com*

"I have never worked a day in my life without selling. If I believe in something, I sell it, and I sell it hard."
Estee Lauder *(1906 – 2004) American founder of Estee Lauder Companies*

"There's a place in the world for any business that takes care of its customers - after the sale."
Harvey MacKay *(1932 -) American writer & businessperson*

"In sales, a referral is the key to the door of resistance."
Bo Bennett *American writer & businessperson*

"Follow the customer, if they change… we change."
Terry Leahy *(1956 -) British businessperson*

"Every sale has five basic obstacles: no need, no money, no hurry, no desire, no trust."
Zig Ziglar *(1926 – 2012) American salesman, author & motivational speaker*

"If you make customers unhappy in the physical world, they might each tell 6 friends. If you make customers unhappy on the Internet, they can each tell 6,000 friends."
Jeff Bezos *(1964 -) American founder of Amazon.com*

"People don't buy for logical reasons – they buy for emotional reasons."
Zig Ziglar *(1926 – 2012) American salesman, author & motivational speaker*

"Do what you do so well that they will want to see it again and bring their friends."
Walt Disney *(1901 – 1966) American founder The Walt Disney Company*

"It is not the employer who pays the wages. Employers only handle the money... It is the customer who pays the wages."
Henry Ford *(1863 – 1947) American founder of the Ford Motor Company*

"The customer's perception is your reality."
Kate Zabriskie *American writer & businessperson*

"The sale begins when the customer says yes."
Harvey MacKay *(1932 -) American writer & businessperson*

"If we don't take care of our customers someone else will."
Unknown

"You can't build a reputation on what you're going to do."
Henry Ford *(1863 – 1947) American founder of the Ford Motor Company*

"People don't want quarter-inch drills. They want quarter inch holes."
Theodore Levitt *(1925 – 2006) American economist & academic*

Learning & Education

Editor's Note:
We were not born complete and we are not complete now, when we recognise this we will soon realise how important continual learning and education is to our entrepreneurial success. We must grow in our leadership role and take on new skills while opening our minds to new attitudes, opinions and thought processes. The following quotes describe different attitudes to education and learning and can help shape your own view on the topic.

"Invest in yourself, in your education. There's nothing better."
Sylvia Porter *(1913 – 1991) American economist & journalist*

"Formal education will make you a living. Self-education will make you a fortune."
Jim Rohn *(1930 – 2009) American motivational speaker & author*

"An investment in knowledge always pays the best interest."
Benjamin Franklin *(1706 - 1790) American president & polymath*

"Education costs money, but then so does ignorance."
Claus Moser *(1922 -) British statistician*

"You can't learn in school what the world is going to do next year."
Henry Ford *(1863 – 1947) American founder of the Ford Motor Company*

"The roots of education are bitter, but the fruit is sweet."
Aristotle *(384 – 322 BCE) Greek philosopher & polymath*

"Tell me and I'll forget; show me and I may remember; involve me and I'll understand." **Chinese proverb**

"Education is what remains after one has forgotten everything he learned in school."
Albert Einstein *(1879 – 1955) Swiss-American Nobel-laureate physicist*

"Anyone who stops learning is old, whether twenty or eighty. Anyone who keeps learning stays young. The greatest thing you can do is keep your mind young."
Mark Twain *(1835 – 1910) American author & humourist*

"Be a life long student, read as many books as possible."
Nelson Mandela *(1918 -) South African president & civil rights leader*

"I learn as much from a turtle as from a religious text."
Dalai Lama the 14th *(1935 -) Tibetan leader of Tibetan Buddhism*

"No matter how busy you may think you are, you must find time for reading, or surrender yourself to self-chosen ignorance."
Confucius *(551 – 479 BCE) Chinese philosopher*

"The illiterates of the 21st century will not be those who cannot read and write but those who cannot learn, unlearn, and relearn."
Alvin Toffler *(1928 -) American writer & futurist*

"You cannot teach a man anything. You can only help him discover it within himself."
Galileo Galilei *(1564 – 1642) Italian scientist, philosopher & polymath*

"Develop a passion for learning. If you do, you will never cease to grow."
Anthony J. D'Angelo *American founder of Collegiate EmPowernet*

"The mind is not a vessel to be filled, but a fire to be kindled."
Plutarch *(46 – 120) Greek-Roman historian and writer*

"We all are learning, modifying, or destroying ideas all the time. Rapid destruction of your ideas when the time is right is one of the most valuable qualities you can acquire. You must force yourself to consider arguments on the other side."
Charlie Munger *(1924 -) American investor, Vice-Chairman Berkshire Hathaway & Chairman Wesco Financial*

"The only true wisdom is knowing that you know nothing."
Socrates *(469 – 399 BCE) Greek philosopher*

"I've learned that mistakes can often be as good a teacher as success."
Jack Welch *(1935 -) American businessperson*

"A college education should equip one to entertain three things: a friend, an idea and oneself."
Thomas Ehrlich *Academic*

"If I'm setting up a new business I'll spend three or four months learning everything there is about that business, everything there is about that subject and then I will find good people to run it on a day-to-day basis, but whilst they're running it at least I know what they're talking about when they come back to me."
Richard Branson *(1950 -) British founder of Virgin Group*

"I have never let my schooling interfere with my education."
Mark Twain *(1835 – 1910) American author & humourist*

"Watch, listen, and learn. You can't know it all yourself - anyone who thinks that they do is destined for mediocrity."
Donald Trump *(1946 -) American founder of The Trump Organisation and Trump Entertainment Resorts*

"Those who do not study are only cattle dressed up in men's clothes."
Chinese Proverb

"If the only tool you have is a hammer, you tend to see every problem as a nail."
Abraham Maslow *(1908 – 1970) American psychologist*

"I never learn anything talking. I only learn things when I ask questions."
Lou Holtz *(1937 -) American football coach and motivational speaker*

"Learning is a treasure that will follow its owner everywhere."
Chinese Proverb

Planning & Organisational Strategy

Editor's Note:
Being able to articulate a strategy and plan is one of the first steps you must take as an entrepreneur, and then continually monitoring and updating these will be just as important. Your idea and business is obviously based on a vision you have on what will occur in the future, and being able to achieve this vision and reach your goals is the benefit of having good plans and strategies. These quotes will remind you how important these processes and skills are and guide you through your own developments.

"Lack of direction, not lack of time, is the problem. We all have twenty-four hour days."
Zig Ziglar *(1926 – 2012) American salesman, author & motivational speaker*

"The best time to plant a tree was 20 years ago. The second best time is now."
Chinese Proverb

"Strategy is not the consequence of planning, but the opposite: its starting point."
Henry Mintzberg *(1939 -) Canadian academic & author*

"One important key to success is self-confidence. An important key to self-confidence is preparation."
Arthur Ashe *(1943 – 1993) American tennis player*

"No wind is of service to him that is bound for nowhere."
French Proverb

"You don't need to have a 100-person company to develop that idea."
Larry Page *(1973 -) American founder of Google*

"A good plan, violently executed now, is better than a perfect plan next week."

George S. Patton *(1885 – 1945) American general*

"Everyone has a plan - until they get punched in the face."
Mike Tyson *(1966 -) American boxer*

"First comes thought; then organisation of that thought, into ideas and plans; then transformation of those plans into reality. The beginning, as you will observe, is in your imagination."
Napoleon Hill *(1883 – 1970) American author & motivational speaker*

"Planning is bringing the future into the present so that you can do something about it now."
Alan Lakein *American author*

"The general who wins the battle makes many calculations in his temple before the battle is fought. The general who loses makes but few calculations beforehand."
Sun Tzu *(544 – 496 BCE) Chinese general*

"He, who could foresee affairs three days in advance would be rich for thousands of years."
Chinese Proverb

"We don't have a traditional strategy process, planning process like you'd find in traditional technical companies. It allows Google to innovate very, very quickly, which I think is a real strength of the company."
Eric Schmidt *(1955 -) American engineer & businessperson*

"When I have one week to solve a seemingly impossible problem, I spend six days defining the problem. Then, the solution becomes obvious."
Albert Einstein *(1879 – 1955) Swiss-American Nobel-laureate physicist*

"Do not repeat the tactics which have gained you one victory, but let your methods be regulated by the infinite variety of circumstances."
Sun Tzu *(544 – 496 BCE) Chinese general*

"Planning is bringing the future into the present so that you can do

something about it now."
Alan Lakein *American author*

"What's the use of running if you are not on the right road."
German proverb

"As for the future, your task is not to foresee it, but to enable it."
Antoine de Saint-Exupery *(1900 – 1944) French writer and aviator*

"Before you journey, observe the wind carefully, detect its direction, and then follow it. You will get to your destination twice as fast with half the effort."
Chin-Ning Chu *(1947 – 2009) Chinese-American businessperson & author*

"Strategy without tactics is the slowest route to victory. Tactics without strategy is the noise before defeat."
Sun Tzu *(544 – 496 BCE) Chinese general*

"Reduce your plan to writing. The moment you complete this, you will have definitely given concrete form to the intangible desire."
Napoleon Hill *(1883 – 1970) American author & motivational speaker*

"Someone's sitting in the shade today because someone planted a tree a long time ago."
Warren Buffett *(1930 -) American investor & Chairman Berkshire Hathaway*

"A pint of sweat will save a gallon of blood."
George S. Patton *(1885 – 1945) American general*

"Nothing is permanent, but change."
Heraclitus *(535–475 BC) pre-Socratic Ionian philosopher*

"The essence of strategy is choosing what not to do."
Michael E. Porter *(1947 -) American academic*

"One of the things that is most important for a company is to be very clear about their strategy, so investors get to self-select as to whether

or not that's the right strategy for them."
Jeff Bezos *(1964 -) American founder of Amazon.com*

"To be prepared is half the victory."
Miguel De Cervantes *(1547-1616) Spanish novelist, dramatist & poet*

"Thinking well is wise; planning well, wiser; but doing well is the wisest and best of all."
Persian Proverb

"However beautiful the strategy, you should occasionally look at the results."
Winston Churchill *(1874 – 1965) British prime minister*

Negotiation & Persuasion

Editor's Note:
Whether it is with financiers, or with suppliers or customers, or others, you will need to be able to negotiate confidently and effectively in your business. This is a balancing act of communication and teamwork and an often-daunting exercise. You will need to know when to give ground and when to put your foot down. The following quotes will give you confidence and advice on how to become skilled in this critical business skill.

"My father said: You must never try to make all the money that's in a deal. Let the other fellow make some money too, because if you have a reputation for always making all the money, you won't have many deals."
J. Paul Getty *(1892 – 1976) American founder of Getty Oil Company*

"Only free men can negotiate. Prisoners cannot enter into contracts."
Nelson Mandela *(1918 -) South African president & civil rights leader*

"The single and most dangerous word to be spoken in business is no. The second most dangerous word is yes. It is possible to avoid saying either."
Lois Wyse *(1926 – 2007) American businessperson & author*

"I'd like to add that negotiating is not something to be avoided or feared - it's an everyday part of life."
Leigh Steinberg *(1949 -) American sports agent*

"Start out with an ideal and end up with a deal."
Karl Albrecht *(1920 -) German founder of Aldi*

"If you wish to win a man over to your ideas, first make him your friend."
Abraham Lincoln *(1808 – 1865) American president*

"Never forget the power of silence, that massively disconcerting pause which goes on and on and may at last induce an opponent to babble

and backtrack nervously."
Lance Morrow *(1939 -) American writer*

"In business as in life, you don't get what you deserve, you get what you negotiate." **Chester L. Karrass** *American businessperson & author*

"Whoever most vividly characterizes a situation usually determines how others see it, talk about it, and make decisions about it."
Kare Anderson *Journalist & author*

"He makes people pleased with him by making them first pleased with themselves."
Earl of Chesterfield (Unknown) *British peer*

"If you would persuade, you must appeal to interest rather than intellect."
Benjamin Franklin *(1706 - 1790) American president & polymath*

"When a man says that he approves something in principal, it means he hasn't the slightest intention of putting it in practice."
Otto Von Bismarck *(1815 – 1898) Prussian statesperson*

"He who wants to persuade should put his trust not in the right argument, but in the right word. The power of sound has always been greater than the power of sense."
Joseph Conrad *(1857 – 1924) Polish-British author*

"That which we do not believe, we cannot adequately say; even though we may repeat the words ever so often."
Ralph Waldo Emerson *(1803 – 1882) American writer & lecturer*

"The most important persuasion tool you have in your entire arsenal is integrity."
Zig Ziglar *(1926 – 2012) American salesman, author & motivational speaker*

"If I have said something to hurt a man once, I shall not get the better of this by saying many things to please him."
Samuel Johnson *(1709 – 1784) English writer*

"You're in a much better position to talk with people when they approach you than when you approach them."
Peace Pilgrim *(1908 – 1981) American spiritual teacher & activist*

"One of the best ways to persuade others is with your ears – by listening to them."
Dean Rusk *(1909 – 1984) American statesperson*

"Before you try to convince anyone else, be sure you are convinced, and if you cannot convince yourself, drop the subject."
John H. Patterson *(1844 – 1922) American founder of National Cash Register Company*

"He who has learned to disagree without being disagreeable has discovered the most valuable secret of a diplomat."
Robert Estabrook *(? – 2011) American journalist & publisher*

"You can get much farther with a kind word and a gun that you can with a kind word alone."
Al Capone *(1899 – 1947) American gangster*

"The truth isn't the truth until people believe you, and they can't believe you if they don't know what your saying, and they can't know what you've saying if they don't listen to you, and they won't listen to you if you're not interesting, and you won't be interesting until you say things imaginatively, originally, freshly."
William Bernbach *(1911 – 1982) American advertiser*

"The most important trip you may take in life is meeting people half way."
Henry Boyle *(1833 – 1890) British peer & diplomat*

"Never cut what you can untie."
Joseph Joubert *(1754 – 1824) French moralist and writer*

"Flattery is the infantry of negotiation."
Lord Chandos *(1893 – 1972) British businessperson and politician*

"More flies are caught with honey than with vinegar."
French Proverb

"If you are planning on doing business with someone again, don't be too tough in the negotiations. If you're going to skin a cat, don't keep it as a house cat."
Unknown

"It is easy to know when a government wishes for peace by observing the character of the person sent to negotiate for it."
Napoleon Bonaparte *(1769 – 1821) French emperor*

"The unforgivable crime is soft hitting. Do not hit at all if it can be avoided; but never hit softly."
Theodore Roosevelt *(1858 – 1919) American president*

Ethics & Responsibility

Editor's Note:
With a successful business comes responsibility. Some of history's greatest entrepreneurs have left tremendous legacies outside of their immediate families, and it is time to start thinking about the legacy you want to leave. Even before leaving a legacy, your business may soon wield immense power and you need to start thinking of how you wish to wield this blessing. Beyond your business' impact, you must decide on how you want to achieve your business goals and the ethics behind this. The next quotes should hopefully remind you of your corporate responsibility and shape the type of businessperson you will become.

"How you climb a mountain is more important than reaching the top."
Yvon Chouinard *(1938 -) American founder of Patagonia*

"After the game, the king and the pawn go into the same box."
Italian proverb

"He that does good to another does good also to himself."
Lucius Annaeus Seneca *(ca. 4BC-65AD) Roman Stoic philosopher, statesman and dramatist*

"The best way to make happy money is to make money your hobby and not your god."
Scott Alexander *American Author*

"Integrity is what we do, what we say and what we say we do."
Don Galer *Businessperson*

"The price of greatness is responsibility."
Winston Churchill *(1874-1965) British prime minister*

"If you don't have integrity, you have nothing. You can't buy it. You can have all the money in the world, but if you are not a moral and ethical person, you really have nothing."
Henry Kravis *(1944 -) American founder of Kohlberg Kravis Roberts*

& Co.

"The test of our progress is not whether we add more to the abundance of those who have much; it is whether we provide enough for those who have too little."
Franklin D. Roosevelt *(1882-1945) American president*

"In London, Washington, and Paris people talk of bonuses or no bonuses. In parts of Africa, South Asia, and Latin America, the struggle is for food or no food."
Robert Zoellick *(1953–) American president of the World Bank*

"It is never too late to be who you might have been."
George Eliot *(1819 – 1880) English writer*

"It is not good enough to do what the law says. We need to be in the forefront of these [social responsibility] issues."
Anders Dahlvig *(1957 -) Swedish businessperson*

"Focusing your life solely on making a buck shows a certain poverty of ambition. It asks too little of yourself… Because it's only when you hitch your wagon to something larger than yourself that you realize your true potential."
Barack Obama *(1961 -) American president*

"The time is always right to do what is right."
Martin Luther King Jr. *(1929-1968) American civil rights leader & Nobel Peace Prize laureate*

"I resolved to stop accumulating and begin the infinitely more serious and difficult task of wise distribution."
Andrew Carnegie *(1835 – 1919) Scottish-American founder of Carnegie Steel Company & philanthropist*

"Being good is good business."
Anita Roddick *(1942 – 2007) British founder of The Body Shop*

"To see what is right and not to do it is want of courage."
Confucius *(551 – 479 BCE) Chinese philosopher*

"Live so that when your children think of fairness and integrity, they

think of you."
H. Jackson Brown, Jr. *American author*

"To sin by silence when they should protest makes cowards of men."
Abraham Lincoln *(1808 – 1865) American president*

"If ethics are poor at the top, that behavior is copied down through the organization."
Robert Noyce *(1927 – 1990) American founder of Fairchild Semiconductor and Intel*

"The most important thing for a young man is to establish a credit… a reputation, character."
John D. Rockefeller *(1839 – 1937) American founder of Standard Oil & philanthropist*

"Have the courage to say no. Have the courage to face the truth. Do the right thing because it is right. These are the magic keys to living your life with integrity."
W. Clement Stone *(1902 – 2002) American author & businessperson*

"There's no such thing as business ethics; there's just ethics. And ethics makes no concessions for the real or imagined necessities of making a profit."
Michael S. Josephson *(1942 -) American founder of Joseph and Edna Josephson Institute of Ethics*

"It has become dramatically clear that the foundation of corporate integrity is personal integrity."
Samuel DiPiazza *American businessperson*

"Real integrity is doing the right thing, knowing that nobody's going to know whether you did it or not."
Oprah Winfrey *(1954 -) Founder & CEO Harpo Productions & Oprah Winfrey Network*

"You must take personal responsibility. You cannot change the circumstances, the seasons, or the wind, but you can change yourself. That is something you have charge of."
Jim Rohn *(1930 – 2009) American motivational speaker & author*

"Honesty is the first chapter in the book of wisdom."
Thomas Jefferson *(1743 – 1826) American president and independence leader*

"We have a responsibility to look after our planet. It is our only home."
Dalai Lama the 14th *(1935 -) Tibetan leader of Tibetan Buddhism*

For Women Entrepreneurs

Editor's Note:
Firstly, I am a male, so I can never know the barriers that women have and continue to face solely based on their gender. But I was raised, in a single-parent household, by a super-strong woman who shaped my values towards feminism as well as many other beliefs, so I believe it was important to include this chapter. Entrepreneurship provides tremendous opportunities to women in particular, as in a way, you have the chance to set your own ceiling rather than have it set by others. In the United States (according to Forbes.com) 44% of entrepreneurs are females (and therefore CEOs) and in countries like Singapore and Brazil, female entrepreneurs equal or exceed their male counterparts, in numbers. However, while the opportunities are unlimited and you set the direction, you may still face gender-based hurdles. Therefore these quotes are all from trailblazing women and are aimed at inspiring and motivating you to achieve success while creating more trails for future female businesspeople.

"The person who knows HOW will always have a job. The person who knows WHY will always be his boss."
Diane Ravitch *(1938 -) American educator & academic*

"Courage is like a muscle. We strengthen it by use."
Ruth Gordon *(1896 – 1985) American actor & writer*

"No one can make you feel inferior without your consent"
Eleanor Roosevelt *(1884 – 1962) American first lady*

"When I thought I couldn't go on, I forced myself to keep going. My success is based on persistence, not luck."
Estée Lauder *Founder of Estée Lauder Companies*

"If you think you're too small to have an impact, try going to bed with a mosquito in the room."
Anita Roddick *(1942 – 2007) British Founder of The Body Shop*

"You cannot shake hands with a clenched fist."
Indira Gandhi *(1917 – 1984) Indian prime minister*

"I praise loudly, I blame softly."
Catherine the Great *(1729 – 1796) Russian empress*

"Every time you state what you want or believe, you're the first to hear it. It's a message to both you and others about what you think is possible. Don't put a ceiling on yourself."
Oprah Winfrey *(1954 -) Founder & CEO Harpo Productions & Oprah Winfrey Network*

"Kind words can be short and easy to speak, but their echoes are truly endless."
Mother Teresa *(1910 – 1997) Albanian-Indian founder of the Missionaries of Charity*

"If you don't accept failure as a possibility, you don't set high goals, you don't branch out, you don't try -- you don't take the risk."
Rosalynn Carter *(1927 -) American first lady*

"Courage doesn't always roar. Sometimes courage is the quiet voice at the end of the day saying, 'I will try again tomorrow'."
Mary Anne Radmacher *Author, artist & lecturer*

"Without leaps of imagination, or dreaming, we lose the excitement of possibilities. Dreaming, after all, is a form of planning."
Gloria Steinem *(1934 -) American journalist and activist*

"Trust your instincts."
Estee Lauder *(1906 – 2004) American founder of Estee Lauder Companies*

"I have yet to hear a man ask for advice on how to combine marriage and a career."
Gloria Steinem *(1934 -) American journalist and activist*

"Parents can only give good advice or put them [children] on the right paths, but the final forming of a person's character lies in their own hands."
Anne Frank *(1929-1945) German writer*

"As long as you keep a person down, some part of you has to be

down there to hold him down, so it means you cannot soar as you otherwise might."
Marian Anderson *(1897 – 1993) American singer*

"A strong woman understands that the gifts such as logic, decisiveness, and strength are just as feminine as intuition and emotional connection. She values and uses all of her gifts."
Unknown

"Anything's possible if you've got enough nerve."
J.K Rowling *(1965 -) British writer*

"Whatever women do they must do twice as well as men to be thought half as good. Luckily, this is not difficult."
Charlotte Whitton *(1896 – 1975) Canadian politician*

"Instead of thinking about where you are, think about where you want to be. It takes twenty years of hard work to become an overnight success."
Diana Rankin *Author & lecturer*

"If you realized how powerful your thoughts are, you would never think a negative thought."
Peace Pilgrim *(1908 – 1981) American spiritual teacher & activist*

"The most effective way to do it, is to do it."
Amelia Earhart *(1897 – 1937) American aviator*

"I am not afraid…I was born to do this."
Joan of Arc *(1412 – 1431) French military leader*

"The question isn't who's going to let me; it's who is going to stop me."
Ayn Rand *(1905 – 1982) Russian-American writer & philosopher*

"An actress can only play a woman. I'm an actor, I can play anything."
Whoopi Goldberg *(1955 -) American actor, artist and writer*

"You only live once, but if you do it right, once is enough."
Mae West *(1893 – 1980) American actor & writer*

"I've learned that people will forget what you said, people will forget what you did, but people will never forget how you made them feel."
Maya Angelou *(1928 -) American author & poet*

"Don't compromise yourself. You are all you've got."
Janis Joplin *(1943 – 1970) American singer & songwriter*

"The most courageous act is still to think for yourself. Aloud."
Coco Chanel *(1883 – 1971) French founder of Chanel*

Humour & Laughter

Editor's Note:
Now to the final chapter, and since the whole book has been somewhat heavy and serious, it is time to have a laugh and look at the lighter side of entrepreneurship and business. It's always important to be able to laugh at yourself and remember that your business may not be the only meaning to life. So enjoy these quotes and have a giggle, while remembering to not always take things too seriously.

"There's no business like show business, but there are several businesses like accounting."
David Letterman *(1947 -) American TV personality & comedian*

"A lot of people become pessimists from financing optimists."
Unknown

"My son is now an 'entrepreneur'. That's what you're called when you don't have a job."
Ted Turner *(1938 -) American founder of CNN*

"A bank is a place that will lend you money if you can prove that you don't need it."
Bob Hope *(1903 – 2003) English-American comedian & actor*

"Experience is simply the name we give our mistakes."
Oscar Wilde *(1854 – 1900) Irish writer & poet*

"How many people on their deathbed wish they'd spent more time at the office?"
Stephen R. Covey *(1932 – 2012) American businessperson, lecturer & writer*

"Litigation is the basic legal right which guarantees every corporation its decade in court."
David Porter *American businessperson*

"You say: 'I'm bright and ambitious.' Investor thinks: 'That's a relief because I usually invest in stupid and lazy people.'"

Guy Kawasaki *(1954 -) American author, lecturer, investor & businessperson*

"Money, it turned out, was exactly like sex, you thought of nothing else if you didn't have it and thought of other things if you did."
James Baldwin *(1924 – 1987) American writer*

"If you can count your money, you don't have a billion dollars."
J. Paul Getty *(1892 – 1976) American founder of Getty Oil Company*

"I like work; it fascinates me. I can sit and look at it for hours."
Jerome K. Jerome *(1859 – 1927) English writer & humourist*

"Always forgive your enemies. Nothing annoys them more."
Oscar Wilde *(1854 – 1900) Irish writer & poet*

"When a man tells you he got rich through hard work, ask him whose?"
Don Marquis *(1878 – 1937) American humourist & writer*

"I learned that sometimes when a lot of people say you're wrong, you may actually be wrong."
John Katzman *(1959 -) Founder of The Princeton Review, 2U and Noodle Education*

"Accept that some days you're the pigeon, and some days you're the statue."
Scott Adams *(1957 -) American creator of 'Dilbert' comic strip*

"You say: 'My goal is to build a world-class company.' Investor thinks: 'How about you ship and sell the first copy before we talk about world-class anything?'"
Guy Kawasaki *(1954 -) American author, lecturer, investor & businessperson*

"When you've got 5 minutes to fill, Twitter is a great way to fill 35 minutes."
Matt Cutts *Computer scientist & businessperson*

"Entrepreneurship is the last refuge of the trouble making individual."

Natalie C. Barney *(1876 – 1972) American writer*

"Don't worry about people stealing your ideas. If your ideas are any good, you'll have to ram them down people's throats."
Howard Aiken *(1900 – 1973) American computer engineer*

"I've got all the money I'll ever need if I die by four o'clock this afternoon."
Henry Youngman *(1906 – 1998) British-American comedian & violinist*

"There's no secret about success. Did you ever know a successful man who didn't tell you about it?"
Kin Hubbard *(1968 – 1930) American humourist, cartoonist & journalist*

"Every successful enterprise requires three men – a dreamer, a businessman, and a son-of-a-bitch."
Unknown

"You don't want another Enron? Here's your law: If a company, can't explain, in ONE SENTENCE...what it does...it's illegal."
Lewis Black *(1948 -) American comedian, writer & actor*

"Anyone who lives within their means suffers from a lack of imagination."
Oscar Wilde *(1854 – 1900) Irish writer & poet*

"One of the symptoms of an approaching nervous breakdown is the belief that one's work is terribly important."
Bertrand Russell *(1872 – 1870) British philosopher, mathematician and historian*

Final Quote for Inspiration

Our deepest fear is not that we are inadequate.
Our deepest fear is that we are powerful beyond measure.
It is our light, not our darkness
That most frightens us.

We ask ourselves
Who am I to be brilliant, gorgeous, talented, fabulous?
Actually, who are you not to be?
You are a child of God.

Your playing small
Does not serve the world.
There's nothing enlightened about shrinking
So that other people won't feel insecure around you.

We are all meant to shine,
As children do.
We were born to make manifest
The glory of God that is within us.

It's not just in some of us;
It's in everyone.

And as we let our own light shine,
We unconsciously give other people permission to do the same.
As we're liberated from our own fear,
Our presence automatically liberates others.

Marianne Williamson *(1952 -) American spiritual teacher, author & lecturer*

Extras

Book Excerpt

While not covered in this book, financial literacy and the ability to read your own business' financial statements is very important to find out how your business is performing and positioned financially. As an entrepreneur, you may be interested in learning how to read and understand a balance sheet, one of your three key financial statements. The editor of this book (Axel Tracy) has as part of his core business the training of accounting knowledge and has written an book about learning the balance sheet and its implications.

Written for the novice & non-accountant, **Balance Sheet Basics: From Confusion to Comfort in Under 30 Pages**, is the second book written by Axel Tracy (the editor of Great Quotes for Entrepreneurs).

Below is an excerpt from this book. If you wish to Buy the book, click on the link above Now to be taken to the Amazon Product Page.

Assets
"An asset is a resource controlled by the entity as a result of past events, and from which future economic benefits are expected to flow to the entity"
- IASB Conceptual Framework: Chapter 4 The Framework; paragraph 4.4(a)

The definition above is the 'complicated' definition of an asset, which I mentioned earlier. The definition comes from the International Accounting Standards Board (IASB), a financial accounting standards (rules) organization that sets the standards for all nations who follow international accounting standards.

Breaking the jargon down, the definition is not too complicated. An asset is something that is "controlled" by a business (like a factory) due to a "past" transaction (buying the factory), which causes a flow to the business of "future economic benefits", i.e. income will be derived from using the asset in the future (the factory will produce goods in the future that will be sold for income).

Technically, anything that fits inside the above definition could be called an asset. And these are what sit at the top of the balance sheet.

The key idea is that an asset is acquired and/or held by a business in order to generate, or access, cash from it in the future.

Generally, the convention is that assets are listed in order of liquidity down the balance sheet. That means that the most liquid assets (e.g. cash) sit at the top of the list of assets and the least liquid (perhaps an oil transport tanker) sit at the bottom. The term "liquidity" simply refers to the ability to turn the asset into cash. If the asset is considered highly liquid, then it is easy to convert to cash, if it considered highly illiquid, then it is hard to convert to cash.

Taking on board these key ideas, have a look at the Amazon Inc. balance sheet. What can you deduce from the assets listed in this financial statement? Are the highest asset values located near the top, implying lots of liquid assets? What does each asset value tell you about the Amazon business model, e.g. does it use high levels of equipment fixed assets, or have high levels of accounts receivable?

I cannot stress enough the concept of asking yourself, when you look at the balance sheet, "what does this tell me?" If you spend enough time analyzing the accounts, you can start to draw inferences about the business. For example, I just mentioned testing whether the accounts receivable is high, you could spend time comparing the accounts receivable balance over time (over multiple balance sheets) and test if this asset figure is rising or falling. A fall may mean that the business is improving its collections operations, or maybe that it is tightening its credit policy. When you draw one conclusion, you can often check its validity by looking at other sections of the financial statements.

While this last paragraph is more about financial statement analysis rather than understanding balance sheets, I hope you can appreciate the idea that while this concise book can help you get your head around a balance sheet you can always learn more and get more value from all financial statements.

Current Assets

Now that we've covered the definitions of 'current' and 'assets' we can take a little more time looking at specific current assets.

Remembering that the current assets are the most liquid since they are at the top of the balance sheet, you will soon realize that many current assets are, in fact, monetary in nature. That is, they are defined and measured in terms of currency. Where the Property, Plant & Equipment (a non-current asset) value represents something like a factory in a city, many of the current assets specifically represent a currency value (like 'Cash' or 'Accounts Receivable').

Let's add a quick finance concept before moving onto analyzing current assets...
We mentioned that asset liquidity refers to assets ability to be converted to cash. You may ask why a business would give up liquid assets (which can pay the invoices that come in) for less liquid assets (which may involve a lengthy process before using them to pay the invoices)? The answer lies in the generally accepted principle that a business (or even an individual) gives up liquidity in order to (hopefully) obtain a higher return from the asset. Look at Amazon Inc's top two current assets, 'Cash & Equivalents' and 'Short-Term Investments': now both are highly liquid (they both sit right at the top), but from their order you can see that cash is more liquid than short-term investments. Now that makes sense, you can simply go to your bank and make a withdrawal from Cash today, yet you may need a few days or few weeks to sell the Short-Term Investments and wait for the delayed settlement to realize their cash value. But look what also makes sense: do you expect a higher return from your checking account interest rate (Cash & Equivalents) or from your corporate bonds (Short-Term Investments)? While not specifically fitting into the 'Current Assets' section alone, this lesson is important to remember for the rest of this book and your own balance sheet analysis.

Now with this lesson under our belt, what can we learn from the current assets section of a balance sheet? One, of many, things we can draw is that we can test how 'secure' the business will be at maintaining its operations. As mentioned, you can generally only pay the business' bills with cash, and you only really ever go out of business if you can't pay your bills. So knowing this we can look at the structure of a business' current assets. If 'Inventory' is too high, it may mean that the entity can't sell is stock or maintain optimal stock levels in-store. If 'Accounts Receivable' is too high then it may mean that the entity can't collect its debts adequately. Yet, if the more liquid current assets are too high, then this may mean that the entity is forsaking a higher return on its assets for the sake of having lots of cash and short-term investments. Knowing what to look for, and how to interpret values, will take practice, but even within these past few pages you can begin to start telling the story of the business from what may have been an almost 'foreign' set of line items and values.

Books by Axel Tracy

Balance Sheet Basics: From Confusion to Comfort in Under 30 Pages

An introductory book on reading and understanding the balance sheets of businesses. It helps you take more control of your financial statements.

Buy at Amazon.com

Ratio Analysis Fundamentals: How 17 Financial Ratios Can Allow You to Understand Any Business On the Planet

An introductory book on financial ratio analysis, covering 17 of the major accounting/financial ratios. It helps you to analyse the performance of businesses based on data from the financial statements.

Buy at Amazon.com

Author contact details and Amazon Review Request

You can contact me anytime and for any reason at any of these contact points. Tell me if you enjoyed the book, or if you could suggest anything for the 2nd edition.

Email: **axel@accofina.com**
Facebook: **facebook.com/accofinaDotCom**
Twitter: **@accofina**
Google+: **https://plus.google.com/116290178694312037641/**

Amazon Review Request:

As mentioned in the introduction, I'd love to get an Amazon Review from you if you enjoyed, and got value, from this book.

Positive Amazon Reviews are worth their weight gold and could possibly propel my little business beyond my wildest expectations.

If you did get a positive experience from this book, I'd deeply appreciate it if you could spare a couple of minutes to Rate the book (on this book's Amazon product page) and maybe leave a positive Comment. Thanks again.

www.ingramcontent.com/pod-product-compliance
Lightning Source LLC
Chambersburg PA
CBHW021443170526
45164CB00001B/371